Fluency

5

Voyager

Passport E

ISBN 978-1-4168-0574-8

Printed in the United States of America   08 09 10 11 12 13   DIG   9 8 7 6 5 4 3 2

Table of Contents

Space Exploration

Space Camp 1

The Hubble Telescope: A View from Space 2

Furry Friends in Space 3

Auroras: Nature's Light Show 4

How the Moon Affects Tides on Earth 5

Signs and Symbols

Safe Streets for Everyone 6

But Who Won the Baseball Game? 7

Computer Symbols 8

The Jefferson Memorial: Honoring a Great Man 9

An Early Lunch for a Hungry Bunch 10

Exciting Games

A Message about the X Games 11

Shaun White—The Future Boy of Superpipe 12

Jake Discovers the Thrill of the X Games 13

Hillcross: A Sport of Skill and Daring 14

The History of the Winter X Games 15

Interesting Animals

Come to the Cat Show for a Purr-fect Afternoon 16

The Ant and the Chrysalis 17

What People Can Learn from Dogs 18

Lead and Follow 19

Fighting to Save the Kemp's Ridley Sea Turtles 20

Timed Passage 21

Timed Passage 22

Word List 23

Fluency Practice

 Read the story to each other.

 Read the story on your own.

 Read the story to your partner again. Try to read the story even better.

 Questions? Ask your partner two questions about the story. Tell each other about the story you just read.

Timed Reading

1. When you do a timed reading with your partner, make sure that you have practiced your story and know all the words.

2. When you are ready, tell your partner to start the timer.

3. Read carefully, and your partner will stop you at 1 minute. When you stop, mark your place.

4. Count the total number of words you read.

5. In the back of your Student Book, write the number of words you read and color in the squares on your Fluency Chart.

6. Now switch with your partner.

Space Camp

Programs

Scholarships

Related Links

Home

Learn More

Camp Costs and Fees

Have you ever wondered what it would be like to live in space? Now you can find out. Visit Space Camp for a week of learning and fun. Space Camp lets you eat, sleep, and live like a real space explorer!

Make New Friends

If you enjoy math and like learning about our world, Space Camp might be just right for you. Have fun with other children who share your interest in space travel. Together as a crew, you will learn teamwork. You will be encouraged to carry out your very own space task. (94)

Other Activities

There are many fun things to do here. Some campers enjoy our robotics classes. Others like to learn about the history of space travel. They also like feeling weightless in our zero-gravity chamber. Campers can work together to build model rockets that they launch into the sky.

There's plenty of time for relaxing too. For lunch, campers enjoy the same kinds of food that astronauts eat in space. After a full day of learning and fun, campers like to cool off in our swimming pool.

Start planning your visit to Space Camp today! (190)

The Hubble Telescope:
A View from Space

Throughout time, people have gazed into the night sky. Stars, both bright and dim, captured their imaginations. Then, about 400 years ago, the telescope was invented. The first one was small. People could see distant objects more closely. They even could see craters on the moon.

As larger telescopes were built, stars came into clearer view. Still, there was a problem. No matter how big the instruments were, people could see only so far.

Experts were encouraged when rockets put objects into space. (83) They began to wonder what a telescope could see from there. They thought that it would be able to see a lot more from space.

In 1990, a crew of astronauts set up the Hubble Space Telescope. The Hubble is huge! It is as big as a small house. Getting its power from the sun, the telescope circles Earth at high speed. It travels 5 miles per second. Its job is to explore space. It gathers information about things it finds there.

The Hubble sends back amazing pictures of space. It has helped us learn so much about what is out there. Over time, experts hope to learn even more about space. (195)

Furry Friends in Space

Mrs. Perry's fourth grade class was learning about space travel. The students knew that astronauts had been to space. They knew that they even had walked on the moon. However, they did not know that the first living things in space were animals.

Mrs. Perry explained, "Animals were sent into space before people were. You see, objects have no weight in space. People needed to see how well animals would react to being weightless."

The class did some research. They learned that the Russians were the first to send an animal into Earth's orbit. That animal was a dog. (99) People were encouraged by the results of this trip. After it, many dogs traveled the long distance into space.

Then, the class learned about monkeys in space. Monkeys were chosen for a special reason. They could operate some of the spacecraft's instruments. Two monkeys named Patricia and Mike flew as a crew. They both made it home safely. Their trip was declared a success.

These lessons gave the class a new respect for animals. The students knew that animals help people. Until now, though, they did not know quite how far animals had gone to help them. (196)

Auroras: Nature's Light Show

What Are Auroras?

Look toward the northern horizon on a clear night, and you might see a dim glow of lights. These lights are called auroras. They appear as waving sheets of light in the sky and can be different colors. Sometimes they are blue, green, and even purple.

Astronauts have seen the auroras from space. They report that the auroras look like rings of light around the North and South Poles.

How Are Auroras Formed?

Did you know that the sun has a kind of wind? Auroras form when the sun's wind hits the gases in Earth's air. (99)

These gases contain tiny bits of dust, and it actually is this dust that lights up in the night sky. It takes about three days for the sun's wind to reach Earth. If there is a lot of wind, the auroras are especially lovely.

Where Can You See Auroras?

Areas close to either of Earth's poles are the best places to see the auroras. It also is good to be far away from a city because city lights compete with the auroras. Try to find a dark place to watch them. You don't want anything getting in the way of this wonderful light show. (203)

How the Moon Affects Tides on Earth

The moon is Earth's partner as the two bodies travel through space together. The moon affects Earth in many ways. One way has to do with ocean tides.

It takes the moon a little less than a month to circle Earth. As it moves, the moon goes through a series of stages, from new to full. These stages are caused by the way the sun's light falls on the moon's surface. In turn, Earth's tides are caused by the way Earth, the sun, and the moon pull against one another. (90)

When the moon is in its new and full stages, the sun and moon are lined up. Gravity from both the sun and the moon pull against Earth, making the tides high.

When the moon is in its first and last quarter stages, the sun and moon are not lined up. Then, the pull of gravity on Earth's oceans is weaker, and the tides are lower.

People don't have to watch the moon to figure out tides. There are charts that tell exactly when tides will be high or low. One good reason to watch the moon, though, is that it is a beautiful sight in the night sky. (199)

Safe Streets for Everyone

Almost everyone is familiar with traffic signs. They help drivers, bikers, and walkers stay safe on the streets. For years, our leaders have worked on ways to improve these signs. By using certain colors and shapes, they have created signs that give exact messages.

- Red signs mean to stop or to use caution. A red sign with eight sides means stop. A three-sided red sign means to slow down and be ready to stop. It is called a yield sign. This sign used to be yellow. Its color was changed to red to stress its importance. (97)

- Yellow signs with black letters or pictures mean that a dangerous area is ahead. Roadways with special rules also are marked with yellow signs.
- Orange signs with black letters or pictures mean that roadwork is ahead.
- Green signs with white letters show directions or distances to certain places.
- Blue signs show helpful information. Routes to hospitals or camping areas are shown on blue signs.

Whether you walk, ride a bike, roll on skates, or drive a car, traffic signs keep you safe. By checking and obeying these signs, you will stay out of harm's way. (192)

But Who Won the Baseball Game?

The baseball team was bouncing along on the bus. Today's game was out of town. Trey and Josh were bored and wondered how the dull ride could be improved.

When the bus pulled up to a stop sign, Trey was reminded of Street Sign Bingo. He and his teammates had played the game once before, and Trey had won. He was eager to defend his title as champ. He suggested the game, and everyone wanted to play. Josh reminded the players that honesty was important. Everyone had to be truthful about the signs he saw. They created Bingo cards for the game. (102)

As the bus rolled along, Trey saw many familiar signs, and the Bingo card he had made was filling up fast. Suddenly, the bus jerked to a stop. Outside, a herd of cattle milled about in the middle of the road. The driver honked a few times, and the cattle finally moved along.

Just then, both Trey and Josh noticed a sign that said "cattle crossing." Trey glanced at his card and began to smile broadly. Before he could make a mark though, Josh jumped up and yelled, "Bingo!"

"That was quite a battle," laughed Trey. "Let's hope the baseball game is as exciting." (206)

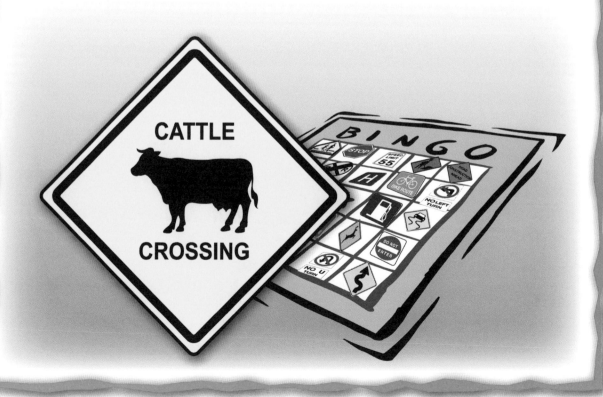

Computer Symbols

Symbols are all around us. They are shapes or marks that stand for something else. They can stand for an object, an idea, or even a sound.

Each letter on this page is a symbol. Letters stand for sounds. When you put the sounds together, they make words. Letters and words are so familiar to us that we rarely think about them as symbols.

Check a computer. You will find a lot of symbols there. The *e* in e-mail stands for electronic. ⑧② We use symbols because they simplify things and improve our lives. Instead of having to write or say electronic mail, it is much easier just to use e-mail.

The symbol @ is another one often used on the computer. It means *at* and is usually found in e-mail addresses. On the keyboard, the number 2 and the @ symbol share the same key. The 2 is shown beneath the @.

Many symbols appear on certain areas of the computer desktop. Some look like folders. Others are colorful designs. These symbols stand for ways in which the computer can be used. ⑱②

The Jefferson Memorial: Honoring a Great Man

In all honesty, our nation's capital is a great place to visit. There is so much to see and do. Visitors can view fine art. They can learn about space and science. They also can learn about our country's history.

In the city, many places recall our country's leaders. Thomas Jefferson is one of those honored. Jefferson wrote the plans for our government. Later, he became our third president.

The place that honors Jefferson was built more than 60 years ago. Before it was built, there were many things to think about. ⑨② People wanted the building to show something about the man. They wanted us to see what he saw. Jefferson liked to design buildings. This one includes many of his ideas. He also enjoyed beautiful gardens. That is why so many different plants can be seen there. Among these are cherry trees that bloom in the spring. They were a gift to our country from Japan.

This building is a memorable place. Come see it at any time of year. ⑰①

An Early Lunch for a Hungry Bunch

Kim's class was visiting the Marine Corps War Memorial for their spring field trip. They had been on the road a long time, and Kim was starting to feel hungry. She heard her stomach growl as she thought about the picnic lunch they had planned.

Suddenly, the bus pulled over and stopped.

"I must have taken a wrong turn," said the bus driver. "I think we're lost. I'll check my directions at that fire station across the street." As her class waited, Mrs. Brown noticed they had stopped near a park.

"We were going to have our picnic when we arrived," she said, "but why don't we eat our lunch right here? This is a lovely park." (117)

While the students enjoyed their lunches, Mrs. Brown told them about what they would see later. She explained that the memorial was a symbol of our country's thankfulness. It was built to honor those who had defended the United States in battle.

Soon, the bus driver came back with the right directions. After finishing lunch, everyone climbed back onto the bus. Before long, the class was on its way. It turned out to be a fun-filled, interesting day. (196)

A Message about the X Games

Folders [Add]

Inbox (1)

Outbox

Sent

Draft

Bulk

Trash

From	Subject
Mountainsports	**X Games Information**

To: Mollyann

From: Mountainsports
Subject: X Games Information

Thank you for your questions about the X Games. I understand that you are writing a research paper and need some information about the Winter X Games. I will be happy to give you some background.

The first Winter X Games happened in 1997. They were held at Big Bear Lake. The main events then were snowboarding and shovel racing. Athletes also competed in ice climbing and bike racing. Today, many more events have been added. There are many different ski competitions. Also, you will find new snowmobile contests. ⑨⑦

Athletes who compete in the X Games spend months or even years in preparation. They know these sports are dangerous. They cannot afford to make mistakes. Of course, the athletes would like to win a medal. Most of all, though, they want to have fun and stay safe.

In 2004, the Winter X Games were held in Aspen, Colorado. More than 300 athletes took part in the games. People from all over the world came to watch them. The weather was cold and even snowy at times. Still, everyone seemed to have a great time.

I hope this will help you with your paper. Maybe you can join us and see the games for yourself next year! ㉑④

Shaun White—The Future Boy of Superpipe

As a small child, Shaun White watched his big brother doing snowboard tricks. He wasn't content to watch for long though. He wanted his brother to teach him to do the tricks. His brother taught him the basics, and Shaun was a natural! He seemed never to have an awkward moment on his snowboard. In a short time, he was doing difficult tricks.

When he was 6 years old, Shaun's parents sent him to snowboard camp. He was the youngest camper there. (82) The coaches saw that Shaun had talent. They knew that with a little improvement, he possibly might become the world's best snowboarder.

It turns out that those coaches were right. All of Shaun's preparation paid off. He became a national champion when he was only 13. At that point, people began calling him "Future Boy." Then, in the 2003 Winter X Games, he won two gold medals. One was in slopestyle. The other was in superpipe. That same year, he became the youngest person ever to win the U.S. Slopestyle Championship. (173)

Jake Discovers the Thrill of the X Games

Jake had never seen skiing like this. He and his father stood at the base of the mountain. They watched skiers glide through the air like acrobats. Since he was little, Jake had watched the Olympics on television. He and his dad liked the skiing best, but those contests were no preparation for the Winter X Games.

Jake was thrilled when he learned the Winter X Games would be held in his town. He never could afford to go to the Olympics. Those games were always in distant places. The travel costs made seeing them in person impossible for most people. Things were different with the X Games. The events were free to attend. (114)

Jake arrived early for the X Games. As he watched the events, Jake hardly could believe his eyes. The skiers were not racing down a hill. Instead, they were doing tricks on special courses. Each course looked like it was designed for a giant skateboard contest.

"How can skiers possibly land those flip-flops and big-air spins?" Jake wondered.

Jake and his dad watched everything, right up to the medal ceremony. Surprisingly, Jake's favorite skier won the gold medal.

"What a day and what a sport!" Jake said with delight as his father drove them home. (211)

Hillcross:
A Sport of
Skill and
Daring

What happens when you combine two of the most extreme winter sports? You get hillcross. Hillcross is a mix of two snowmobile sports. One is the snowcross. The other is the hillclimb.

In hillcross, riders in snowmobiles begin at the bottom of a steep hill. Then, they race one another to the top. Sometimes they reach speeds of 70 miles per hour. Hillcross has very few rules. Because of that, the athletes often take dangerous risks. They soar and glide as they make their way over bumps and jumps to the top of a hill. (95)

Any awkward move can cause the driver to lose the race. The gold medal usually goes to the racer who is best prepared. This often is the athlete who makes the fewest mistakes.

It should be no surprise that hillcross is one of the most popular events at the Winter X Games. As a result, the hillcross course must have room for a lot of racers. It also must have room for the many fans to watch in safety. For those who are fond of excitement, hillcross is definitely a must-see event! (188)

The History of the Winter X Games

The first Winter X Games took place in 1997. Four years earlier, a TV company held the Summer X Games. They were a great success, and the company thought that Winter X Games would be a good idea too. They were right. The first Winter X Games were seen around the world.

Athletes at the first Winter X Games were excited. They would compete in many thrilling events. Snowboarding was popular. So was ice climbing. Some even raced snow shovels. The athletes saw some improvements in game conditions. The courses were much nicer than those they were used to. (99)

At the second Winter X Games, new sports were added. Many of these mixed two of the older events. The new sports drew more notice. Many fans could afford to spend three days at the games, and they found the new events gripping to watch.

The Winter X Games become more and more accepted each year. Today, winning at the games is very special. To some, winning here might be as special as winning at the Olympics. The Winter X Games have thousands of fans, and their popularity shows no sign of slowing down. Neither do the athletes! (197)

Come to the Cat Show for a Purr-fect Afternoon

Saturday, April 3
1:00–5:00 p.m.
Shade Grove Park, Main Building
Organized by Shade City Cat Club

The Shade City Cat Club is happy to announce its annual Cat Show. This will be an especially important show. It marks our group's 20th year in Shade City!

Cat owners are invited to bring their animals. They might want to enter them in the contests. There will be several contest groups. Kittens, purebred cats, and household pets will have a place to compete. Contest rules and entry forms are on our Web site. Printed forms are available at pet stores around town. (100)

You can expect to have a lot of fun. Of course, everyone will want to watch as the cats are judged. Then, you can enjoy a stroll around the lawn. Decorated booths will be set up. All sorts of cat products will be for sale, including special cat foods and health aids. Would your cat look good in a new collar? Colorful, handmade collars will be sold too.

There are two ways to get tickets for the event. Anyone bringing three cans of cat food will be admitted at the door. Others may buy advance tickets at Garza's Pet Store. The entire amount raised from ticket sales will be donated to the animal shelter. (214)

The *Ant* and the *Chrysalis*

The sun was shining brightly, and a soft breeze stirred the grass. Ant made his way through the meadow, gathering seeds and other bits of food. He came across Chrysalis. This creature was peeking out from under a leaf, her tail slowly wiggling back and forth.

"Poor thing!" exclaimed Ant in dismay. "It's too bad that you are stuck in that crusty shell, only able to wiggle your tail. I can crawl up and down the tallest trees. I can wander about freely and go just about anywhere. I pity you, Chrysalis."

Chrysalis listened to Ant, but she didn't reply. (100)

"Well, I must be on my way," said Ant. He wandered on through the grass.

A few days later, Ant passed by the same place. He hunted for Chrysalis and was surprised to find only an empty shell. Just then, Ant felt a breeze and glanced upward to see a gorgeous butterfly flapping its wings.

"Remember me?" asked Butterfly. "I am happy that you can wander and climb, but I also am wonderfully made!" With that, Butterfly floated away, never to be seen by Ant again. (186)

What People Can Learn from Dogs

Throughout history, people have been especially fond of dogs. These handsome creatures have filled the roles of worker and guard. Dogs also have been companions and pets.

Why are dogs so popular? Perhaps it is because of their worthy traits. In fact, people might do well to study dogs and imitate some of their behavior. This could help them lead healthier, happier lives.

Dogs Find Joy in Simple Things.

A long walk or a game of catch is all that most dogs need to become cheerful. And when a dog is happy, you know it. There is no mistaking the wagging tail and cheerful yap. A pat on the head always adds to a dog's happiness. (116)

Dogs Lead Healthy Lives Naturally.

Most people admit to having busy lives. Busy, working dogs can offer models of healthy living. Dogs take naps when they are tired. Immediately after a nap, they stretch slowly, one leg at a time. Also, dogs eat only what they need to stay healthy. They drink plenty of water throughout the day.

Dogs Are Good Friends.

Dogs run to meet their loved ones, even after a short separation. They are loyal and quick to forgive. Even when it may not be deserved, a dog's love and friendship stay steady. Dogs are sensitive to a loved one having a bad day. They will stay close by and offer comfort. (230)

Lead and Follow

Mother Crab was especially proud of her son, Sandy. She thought Sandy was the smartest young crab on the beach.

"Someday, that boy is going to do great things," Mother Crab thought. "And it's partly because I've done a good job of raising him."

As Mother Crab thought these things, she began to worry. "Maybe I haven't taught Sandy everything he needs to know."

Mother Crab turned her attention toward Sandy. She noticed the way he always was telling the other crabs what to do. "If Sandy is going to get along with others," she thought, "he needs to be able to follow as well as lead."

Mother Crab crawled over to her son. ⑭ "Sandy," she said, "I think you need to work on cooperating with others. I am proud that you are able to lead your friends, but you also must learn how to work together. Sometimes that means listening to and learning from someone else."

"I'll try, Mom," Sandy replied. Mother Crab watched her son throughout the next week. He seemed to be making a serious effort. When Sandy ran up to say that his friend had taught him the best way to find food in the tall grass, Mother Crab grinned. He was well on his way. ㉑⓪

Fighting to Save the Kemp's Ridley Sea Turtles

In the Gulf of Mexico, 100-pound sea turtles glide through the warm waters. They are the Kemp's Ridley sea turtles. They are the smallest of the Gulf sea turtles.

There used to be many of these sea turtles. People thought they would be around forever. By the 1970s, though, they were in danger of dying out. One reason was that the turtles and their eggs were good to eat. People would wait for the turtles to lay their eggs on the beach. Then, they would dig up the eggs to eat or to sell. The turtles themselves also were caught and sold for food. (105) Accidents were another reason for the drop in numbers. Many turtles were caught by accident in shrimp nets. In most cases, they would die before they could be released.

When scientists saw the drop in sea turtle numbers, they were dismayed. The entire population of nesting females dropped to between 500 and 1,000. Since then, people have worked to save the turtles. Laws were passed to make shrimp boats use safer nets. Also, volunteers now watch for turtles to lay their eggs on the beach. Then, they make sure the eggs remain safe until they hatch. With luck, these efforts will help Kemp's Ridley sea turtles return in greater numbers. (215)

The Pony, the Stag, and the Rancher

Pony galloped happily through his own grand mountain pasture. He felt lucky to be a wild horse with freedom to roam as he pleased. Pony felt sorry for horses that were caged behind fences.

One day, while Pony was grazing in his meadow, he spotted Stag nibbling on a berry bush. That bush happened to be Pony's favorite! He glared at Stag from behind a tree and started to worry.

"What if all the animals start moving here?" Pony thought. "I might not have enough room to run freely anymore."

Pony decided to try to run off Stag. He could not do it by himself, though, for Stag was a large animal with huge horns and sharp hooves. (118)

Pony trotted down the mountain to Rancher's house and explained his problem.

"I will help you run off Stag," said Rancher, "but there are certain things that we must do to prepare. First, you must let me place this saddle on your back. I'll need to keep steady upon you as we chase Stag. Second, you must let me put this bit in your mouth so that I can guide you with these reins."

Pony agreed to everything. Soon, Stag was sent away, and Pony asked Rancher to remove the saddle and the bit.

"Not so fast," said Rancher. "I think you will be of great help on my ranch just the way you are right now." (233)

Jeff Corwin: A Friend of the Rain Forest

It's hard to coax most people to take an interest in rain forests. First of all, they seem so distant from most people. Second, they look dark and dangerous. They are filled with snakes and poisonous plants. Dreadful, oversized insects are everywhere. Jeff Corwin is different from most people. He has been concerned about the rain forests since he was a child.

Rain forests produce much of the air you are breathing right now. Jeff learned this fact in grade school. Since then, he has had one main goal. It is to spread the word about the importance of rain forests. In particular, he is interested in the many animals that live there. (113)

Why are these animals important? Jeff wants to help people understand the reasons. Many of the animals there cannot live anywhere else. In fact, these forests are home to half of the animal groups in the world. The animals are necessary for the health of the forest. Each one plays a role in keeping the rain forest in bloom. If even one group died out, it could have a terrible effect on the others. All the other plants and animals living with it could suffer.

Jeff has started clubs for young people. The clubs teach ways to help the rain forests. He believes education is the best way to preserve this precious resource. When people learn about rain forests, they will want to help save them. (239)

Word List

planning	quite
visit	react
view	anything
explore	familiar
wonder	sign
chosen	beneath